Felt biscuits
Ouissi Gresty

To Toby and Jacob
My Reason. My Inspiration.

Published by Morse-Brown Publishing
Series Editor: John Morse-Brown
Photography © Morse-Brown Design Limited
Design & Production: Morse-Brown Design Limited.
↗ www.morsebrowndesign.co.uk
For more titles in this series, see ↗ www.how2crafts.com

ISBN: 978-0-9550241-9-1

Printed in the UK by John Price Printers

This is more than just a book...

This is the start of a conversation about making felt sculptures. By buying this book, you've joined that conversation, and we'd love to hear from you...

In this book you'll find photographic step-by-step instructions that will enable you to make a range of classic British biscuits and a biscuit tin, all out of felt. But unlike most craft books you buy, it doesn't stop there. Once you've had a go at making these felt biscuits yourself, (and maybe designed a few different types!), you can upload and share photos of your creations, and any comments and ideas, onto our website at ↗ **how2crafts.com**. Then, once we've come to the end of each print run for this book, we'll select the best photos and comments and include them in the new edition of the book as a 'reader's appendix' – a source of inspiration and alternative designs for future readers.

As we've said on the how2crafts website, we believe crafts are all about conversation – the passing of skills and techniques from person to person down the ages. And we'd like our books to be part of that conversation.

To join in the conversation visit
↗ **www.how2crafts.com**

Talk to us at
↗ **twitter.com/how2crafts**

Welcome & introduction to felt sculpture

I am a felt confectioner; I sculpt British foods out of sheets of felt. By making something that is usually temporary permanent I hope to make people constantly comforted by food that evokes memories of childhood and makes them feel happy and whole.

There is something magical about taking a flat piece of felt, a few yards of thread and a handful of wadding, and sewing, stuffing and sculpting them into something else. Something that brings back memories, lasts a lifetime and makes people smile. And felt sculpture, unlike real food, has no calories, never goes stale and does not have a sell-by date.

I must warn you, though, it can become seriously addictive!

This book has been designed to show you the stitches and steps needed to sew a set of biscuits and a biscuit tin out of sheets of felt. The sculptures can be made anywhere – at the kitchen table, in an armchair in front of a fire or in a deck chair out in the sun.

The finished set looks fabulous displayed on a cake stand or as part of a display on your table, windowsill or dresser.

I hope you enjoy.

Materials

Felt ① There are quite a few different types of felt on the market – wool, acrylic, blends, and ecofelts. I choose to use ecofelt for most of my work but you can use any kind you choose. For the pieces in this set you will need: two sheets of white, three sheets of silver or light grey, one sheet of Wedgwood or royal blue, one sheet of red, two sheets of dark brown, one sheet of brown, two sheets of biscuit, one sheet of cream, one sheet of pink and one sheet of baby pink.

Stuffing ② You can use polyfill, wool or any other sort of toy stuffing, but I prefer to buy wadding by the metre and pull it apart with my fingers. I find it gives a better feel to the finished sculpture than the softer polyfill or the more dense wool stuffing.

Embroidery thread ③ You will need embroidery thread in white, brown, biscuit, blue, red and pink. I use Anchor but there are many makes out there in arrays of lovely colours. The best way to choose the exact colours for your work is to match them to your felt.

Gold metallic thread ④ There are gold embroidery threads but I find them too stiff so I use Anchor Alcazar Metallic thread.

Invisible thread ⑤ This is hard to use as it has a plastic texture, but it makes fabulous sugar crystal French knots. The one I use is by Coats but try a few different ones to see which one works best for you.

Stabiliser ⑥ Some of the biscuits have patterns embroidered on them, and to transfer the pattern to be embroidered onto the felt, I use stabiliser (see 'transferring patterns on to felt on page 10). Try to find the thinnest stabiliser you can. I buy mine by the metre and don't have a favourite brand.

Cardboard ⑦ You'll need three or four pieces of easily bendable cardboard. You need to make sure it is flexible enough to curve around corners without creasing. Try different weights to see which you can curl best with your fingers.

Tools

- Two needles, one with a small eye large enough to take two or three strands of embroidery thread, and one with an eye large enough to hold six strands.

- A large number of pins. You always need more than you think! I use coloured pearl-headed pins but any pins will work nicely.

- A pair of fabric-cutting scissors.

- A pair of embroidery or nail scissors.

- A pen. Brown works better than black as the ink does not cause as much discolouration of the thread. The thinner the nib the better – mine is 0.5mm.

- A pair of tweezers.

- PVA or fabric glue. I use Stix PVA acid-free glue, but any craft or fabric glue will do. Test the one you choose on your felt first, to make sure it doesn't discolour it.

- A small clean paint brush.

- A small toothed comb.

Techniques and stitches

Before beginning to describe how the biscuits are made, I want to introduce some of the techniques and stitches used throughout this book. If you are familiar with needlework feel free to skip this section.

Transferring patterns onto felt

Most of the biscuits have patterns embroidered on them (and I have included these patterns on pages 26–33). To transfer the pattern onto your felt, cut out a piece of stabiliser to fit the design to be embroidered. Place the stabiliser over the pattern piece and use a pen to trace the design onto the stabiliser from the pattern (Fig 1). Now pin the stabiliser onto the piece of felt to be embroidered and embroider the design through the stabiliser (Fig 2).

When you've finished the embroidery the stabiliser needs to be removed. Some stabilisers are thin enough to pull gently off your design with tweezers, but if yours is not, or you are unsure, start by cutting away the stabiliser with embroidery or nail scissors and then pull it off from between the stitches with tweezers (Fig 3). Try doing a test run with your stabiliser before committing to either method, as which method works best depends on a number of factors – namely the felt, your stitch rigidity and the thickness of your stabiliser.

Your embroidery is now transferred onto your felt (Fig 4).

Starting your stitches

Place your felt pieces together and pin them securely. Knot the end of your embroidery thread, and then draw the threaded needle from the inside of one layer through to the outside so that the knot is left between the two layers.

Seam stitch (also known as whip stitch)

A useful stitch for sewing two pieces of felt together along an edge. Thread two strands of embroidery thread through the eye of your needle, and knot the end, pulling the thread from the middle to the front layer, leaving the knot hidden between the two pieces of felt (see 'Starting your stitches' on page 10). Now bring the needle over to the back layer, directly below where the thread comes out of the front layer (Fig 5). Push the needle through both layers of felt at a 45° angle so the needle and thread appear just in front of the first stitch (Fig 6). Repeat until you have completed your seam (Fig 7).

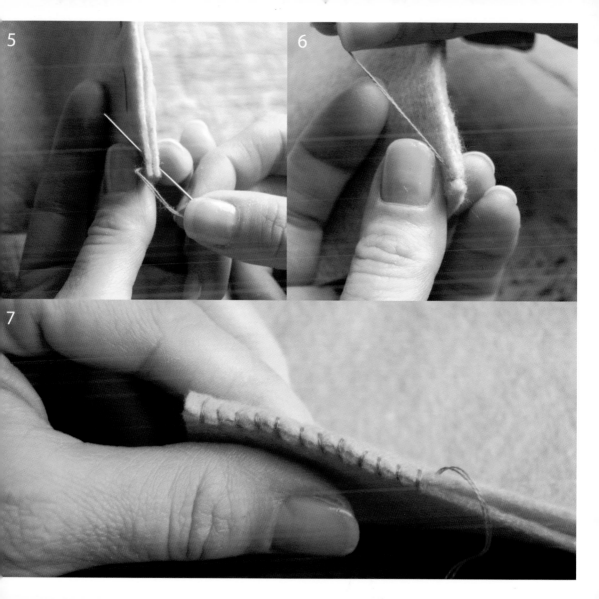

Appliqué stitch

This is the stitch to use when you need to sew one piece of felt on top of another. Thread two strands of embroidery thread through the eye of your needle and knot the end, pulling the thread from the underside of the top layer of felt, just in from the edge, leaving the knot at the back between the two layers (Fig 8). Now push the needle through the lower layer of felt, right at the edge of the top layer of felt, and bring it back up through both layers so the needle appears just in front of the first stitch (Fig 9).

Repeat until you have stitched your top layer onto the bottom layer (Fig 10).

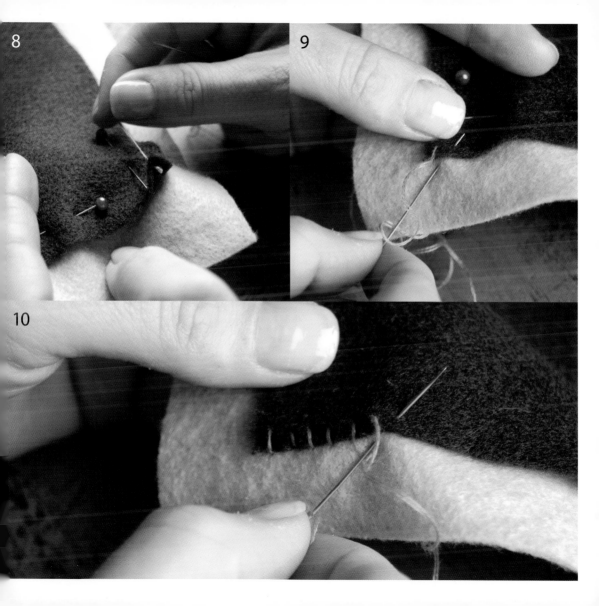

Spot stitch

This is the stitch to use when you want to create a 'dimple' in the surface of a biscuit. Thread six strands of embroidery thread through the eye of your needle and knot the end. Push the needle up from the bottom of the felt to where you wish the dimple to be, leaving the knot at the back (Fig 11). Bring the needle over to the side of the first thread, trying to make the gap between the two threads as small as possible, and draw the thread through to the back (Fig 12). You have created a dimple and the thread should be almost invisible.

Straight stitch

An extremely simple decorative stitch. Thread six strands of embroidery thread through the eye of your needle and knot the end. Push the needle up from the bottom to where you wish to begin your stitch. Bring the needle to where you wish to end the stitch and draw the thread through to the back leaving a single long stitch.

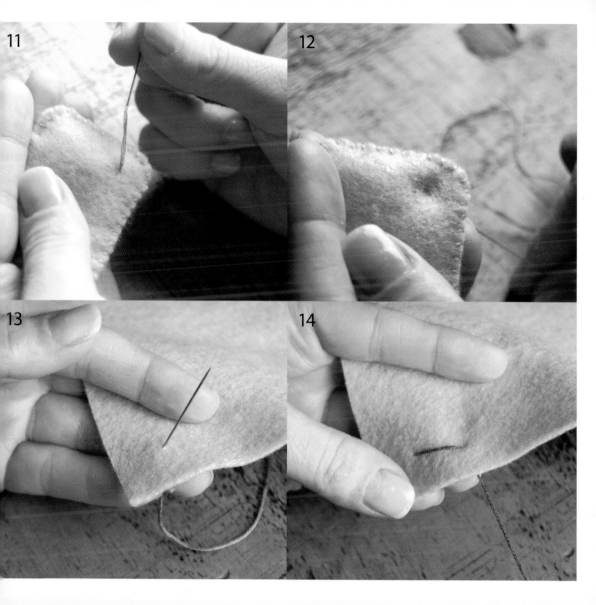

Stem stitch

Another simple decorative stitch. Thread six strands of embroidery thread through the eye of your needle and knot the end. Push the needle up from the back, through the felt layers, just to the left (or right if you are left handed) of your stitch guide line, leaving the knot at the back (Fig 15). Bring the needle over to a point just in front of the initial thread slightly to the right (or left if you are left handed) of the guide line, so the thread sits diagonally over the guide line. Now bring the needle up from the back so it appears immediately to the left of the first stitch (or right if you are left handed) and about half way along it (Fig 16). Repeat until your line is complete (Fig 17).

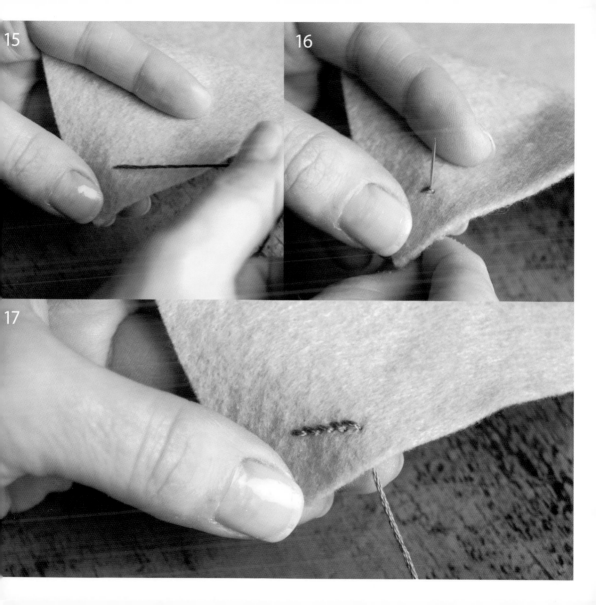

Back stitch

Thread six strands of embroidery thread through the eye of your needle and knot the end. Push the needle up from the back through the felt at the start of your stitch guide line, leaving the knot at the back (Fig 18). Push the needle down through the guide line at the point where you wish to end the first stitch. Now bring the needle up again through the felt so its tip emerges further along the guide line and the gap between the needle and the end of the first stitch is equal to the length of the first stitch (Fig 19). Now push the needle back down again at the point where the first stitch ends (Fig 20), and draw the needle through again from underneath, so it emerges further along the guide line so the gap is again equal to the length of the stitches. Repeat until your line is complete (Fig 21).

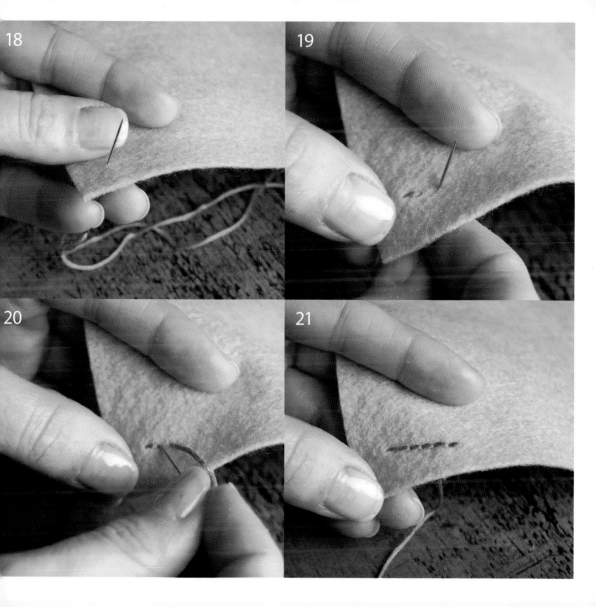

Running stitch

Another simple decorative stitch. Thread two strands of embroidery thread through the eye of your needle and knot the end, pulling the thread through the felt layers at the beginning of your stitch guide line, leaving the knot at the back (Fig 22). Push the needle down through the felt at the point where you wish to end the first stitch (Fig 23). Bring the needle up again through the felt so its tip emerges further along the guide line and the gap between the needle and the end of the first stitch is equal to the length of the first stitch (Fig 24). Repeat until your line is complete (Fig 25).

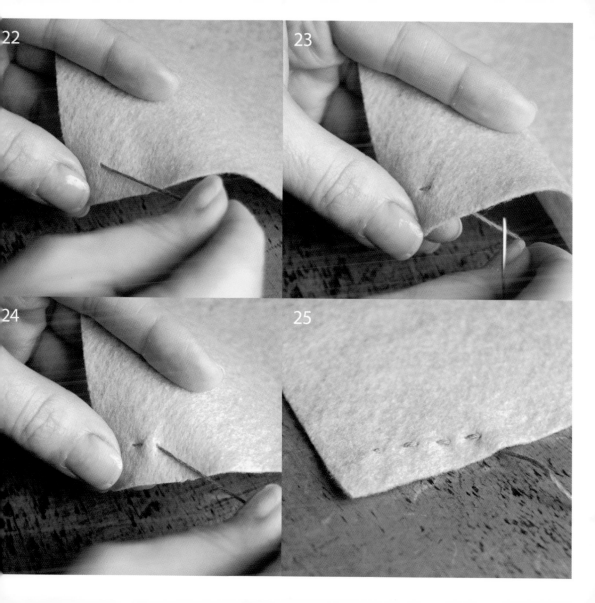

French knots

This is a decorative stitch that produces little raised knots of thread. Thread three strands of embroidery thread through the eye of your needle and knot the end, pulling the thread through the felt where you wish to place the stitch, leaving the knot at the back. Hold the thread down with your left thumb (or right if you're left handed) where it emerges, and wrap the thread three times around the needle (Fig 26). Still holding the thread firmly, bring the needle back to where you started and insert it into the felt as close as possible to the emerging thread (Fig 27). Still holding the thread firmly, push the needle through to the back (Fig 28). Let the thread pull out slowly from under your thumb as the knot starts to form. You now have a small knot on the surface of your felt (Fig 29).

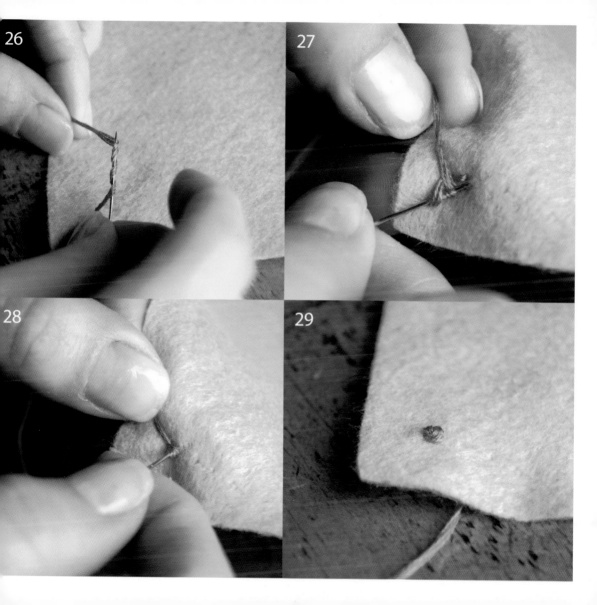

The patterns

Custard Cream body x 4
Colour: *biscuit*

Custard Cream surface design

**Custard Cream
cream x 2
Colour:** *cream*

**Bourbon
body x 4
Colour:
*brown***

Bourbon surface design

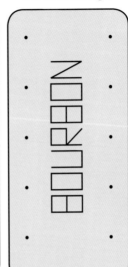

**Bourbon
cream x 2
Colour:
*brown***

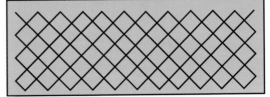

Pink wafer

***Pink* x 5
Baby pink x 6**

**Pink
wafer
surface
design**

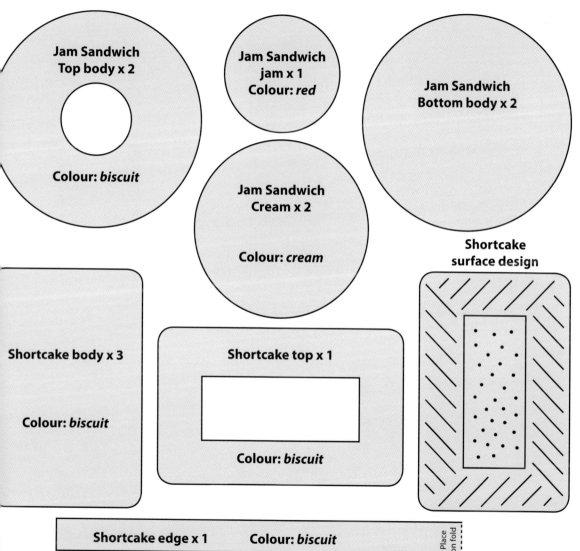

Jam Sandwich
Top body x 2

Colour: *biscuit*

Jam Sandwich
jam x 1
Colour: *red*

Jam Sandwich
Bottom body x 2

Jam Sandwich
Cream x 2

Colour: *cream*

Shortcake
surface design

Shortcake body x 3

Colour: *biscuit*

Shortcake top x 1

Colour: *biscuit*

Shortcake edge x 1   Colour: *biscuit*

Place on fold

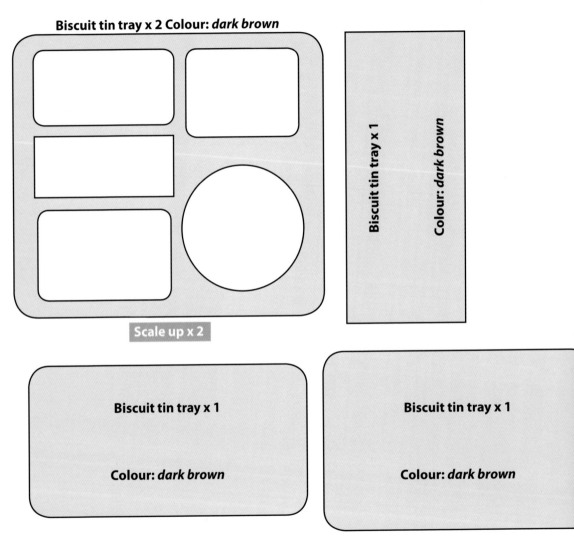

Biscuit tin tray x 2 Colour: *dark brown*

Biscuit tin tray x 1

Colour: *dark brown*

Scale up x 2

Biscuit tin tray x 1

Colour: *dark brown*

Biscuit tin tray x 1

Colour: *dark brown*

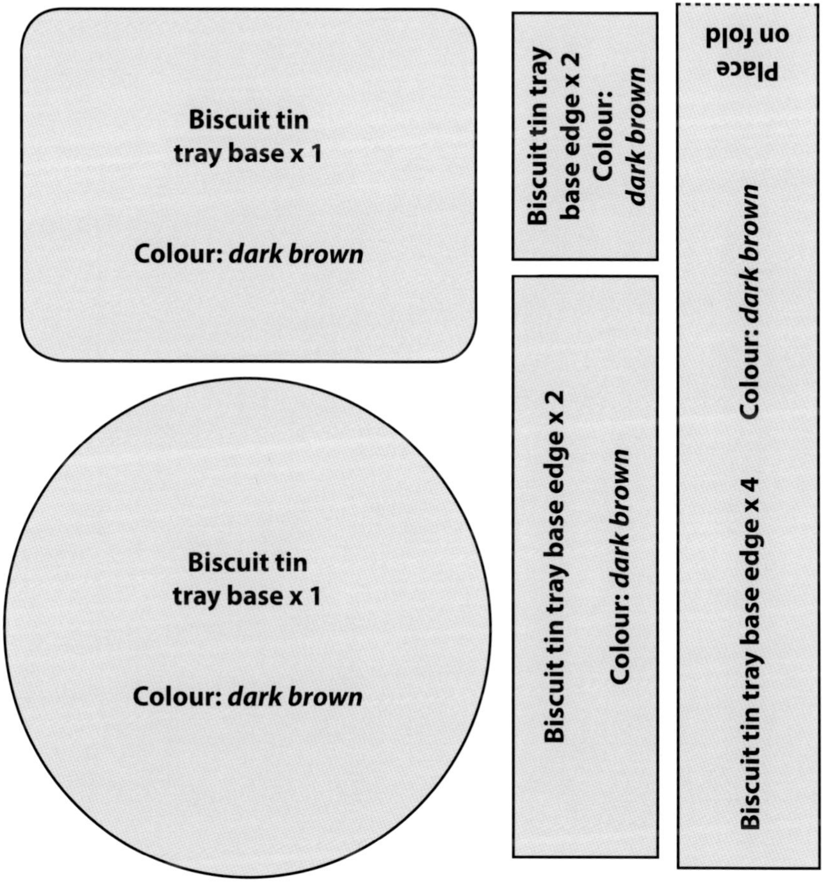

**Biscuit tin
tray base x 1**

Colour: *dark brown*

**Biscuit tin
tray base x 1**

Colour: *dark brown*

**Biscuit tin tray
base edge x 2
Colour:
*dark brown***

Biscuit tin tray base edge x 2

Colour: *dark brown*

**Place
on fold**

Colour: *dark brown*

Biscuit tin tray base edge x 4

Biscuit tin bottom x 2
Colour: *grey*

Biscuit tin top x 1
Card

Scale up x 2

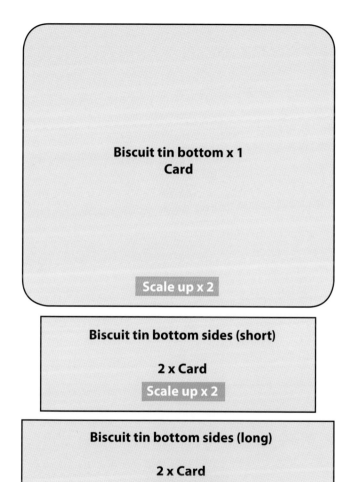

Biscuit tin bottom x 1
Card

Scale up x 2

Biscuit tin bottom sides (short)

2 x Card
Scale up x 2

Biscuit tin bottom sides (long)

2 x Card
Scale up x 2

Biscuit tin top sides (short) 2 x *white* 2 x *grey* Scale up x 2

Biscuit tin top sides (long) 2 x *white* 2 x *grey* Scale up x 2

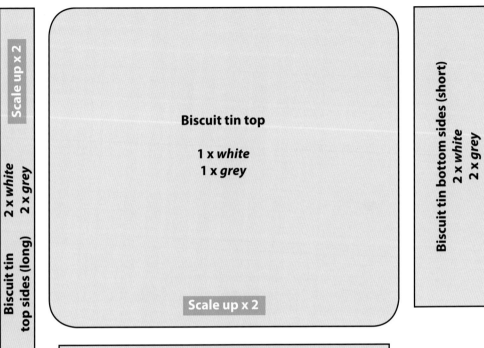

Biscuit tin top

1 x *white*
1 x *grey*

Scale up x 2

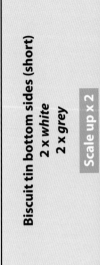

Biscuit tin bottom sides (short) 2 x *white* 2 x *grey* Scale up x 2

Biscuit tin bottom sides (long)
2 x *white*
2 x *grey*

Scale up x 2

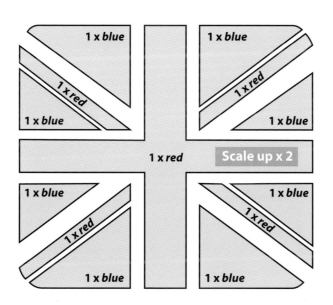

1 x blue

1 x blue

1 x red

1 x red

1 x blue

1 x blue

1 x red

Scale up x 2

1 x blue

1 x blue

1 x red

1 x red

1 x blue

1 x blue

Custard Cream

Cut out the six Custard Cream pattern pieces from page 26 (Fig 30). Sew two of the biscuit body pieces together using seam stitch (page 12), leaving a small gap along one of the shorter edges for stuffing (Fig 31). Stuff with enough stuffing to make the biscuit full and soft but still fairly flat. Sew up the gap (Fig 32).

Now using your stabiliser with the Custard Cream pattern transferred on to it, embroider the double diamond with straight stitch (p16) and the three spots with spot stitch (also p16).

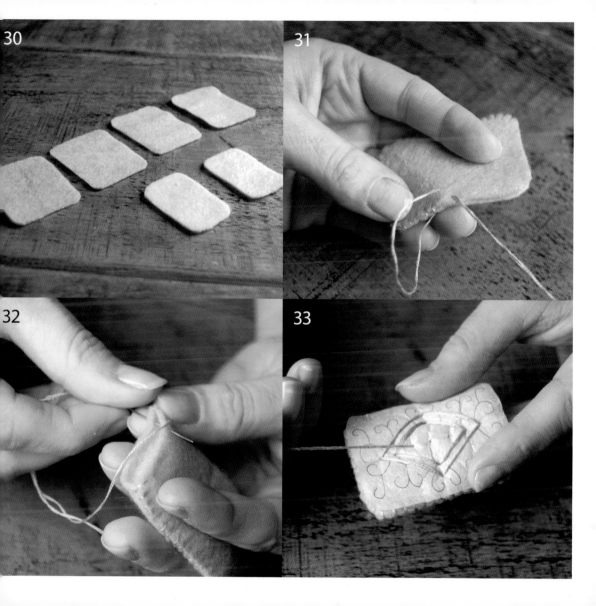

Embroider the curls using stem stitch (Fig 34).
Sew the two custard pieces and one of the
biscuit body pieces (Fig 35) to the underneath of
the embroidered piece with running stitch (Fig
36), making sure the stitches don't show on the
embroidered side of the biscuit.

Sew the last biscuit body piece onto the bottom
as you did for the top two pieces on page 34,
leaving a gap along one of the short sides for
stuffing (Fig 37). Stuff the bottom biscuit so it is
soft and full yet still flat. Sew the gap closed
(Fig 38).

All hail the glorious Custard Cream!

Did you know that the pattern on the top is Baroque? And that nine out of ten people voted Custard Creams to be Britain's favourite biscuit in a poll of 7,000 people?

More information from:
↗ **en.wikipedia.org/wiki/Custard_cream**

Bourbon Biscuit

This is very similar to how the Custard Creams are made, but in case people don't want to make both biscuits, I have included the instructions for each biscuit in full.

Cut out the six Bourbon biscuit pattern pieces from page 26 (Fig 39). Sew two of the biscuit body pieces together using seam stitch (p12), leaving a small gap along one of the shorter edges for stuffing. Stuff with enough stuffing so the biscuit is full and soft but still flat. Sew up the gap (Fig 40).

Now embroider the eight spots along the edges of the biscuit with spot stitches (p16) (Fig 41). Embroider the letter R in the centre of the biscuit using back stitch (p20), then embroider the rest of the letters from the R outwards (Fig 42).

Sew the two chocolate cream pieces and one of the biscuit body pieces (Fig 43) to the underneath of the embroidered piece with running stitch. Make sure the stitching doesn't show on the embroidered surface of the biscuit. Now sew the last biscuit body piece onto the bottom using seam stitch, leaving a gap along one of the short sides for stuffing (Fig 44).

Stuff the bottom biscuit so it is soft and full yet still flat. I use a kebab stick (a pencil will do) to push the stuffing in (Fig 45). Sew the gap closed (Fig 46).

Bow to the Bourbon!

Apparently named after the House of Bourbon, an aristocratic French and Spanish family.

More information from:
↗ **en.wikipedia.org/wiki/Bourbon_biscuit**

Jam Sandwich Cream

Cut out the seven jam sandwich cream pattern pieces from page 27 (Fig 47). Sew the two ring biscuit pieces together leaving a small gap along the outer edge for stuffing (Fig 48). Stuff with enough stuffing so the biscuit is full and soft but still flat. Sew up the gap (Fig 49).

Now take the jam piece and sew around the edge with a loose running stitch (p22) (Fig 50).

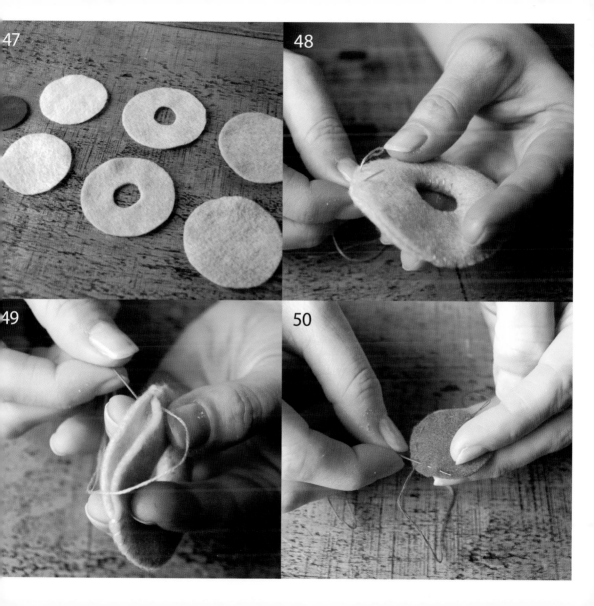

Now pull both ends of the thread until the edges of the jam are gathered, and then tie the ends together with a knot (Fig 51). Stuff loosely (Fig 52) and squash slightly with your thumb so the jam forms a flat stuffed disk with an open back.

Embroider the sugar grains onto the jam layer in invisible thread using French knots (p24) (Fig 53). There isn't a pattern for this – just make about ten spots. Then sew the jam to the edges of the hole in the top biscuit ring (Fig 54).

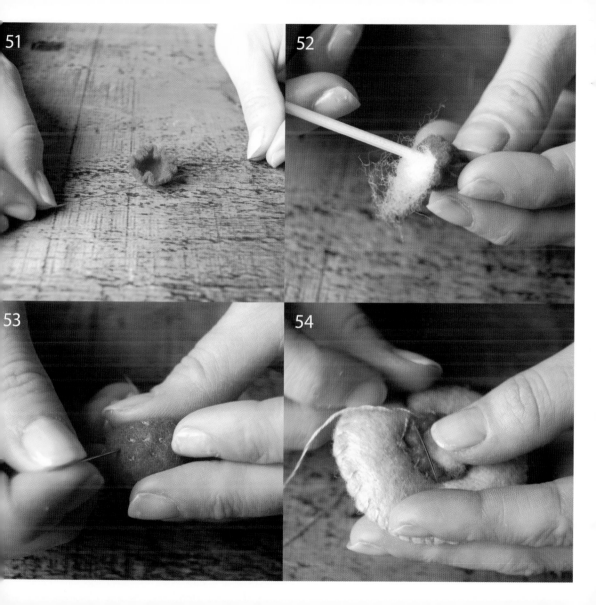

Sew the cream pieces and one of the round biscuit pieces (Fig 55) onto the underneath of the stuffed top ring (Fig 56). Make sure the stitching doesn't show on the top surface of the biscuit.

Sew the second round biscuit piece onto the bottom, leaving a gap for stuffing (Fig 57). Stuff the bottom biscuit so it is soft and full yet still flat. Sew the gap closed (Fig 58).

A resplendent jam sandwich cream!

More information from:
↗ **www.nicecupofteaandasitdown.com/
biscuits/previous.php3?item=19**

Shortcake Biscuit

Cut out the five shortcake pattern pieces from page 27 (Fig 59). Sew two of the biscuit body pieces together leaving a small gap along one of the shorter edges for stuffing (Fig 60). Stuff with enough stuffing so the biscuit is full and soft but still flat. Sew up the gap (Fig 61).

Now sew the inner edge of the shortcake top piece (the one with the hole in the middle) onto the biscuit body with appliqué stitch (Fig 62).

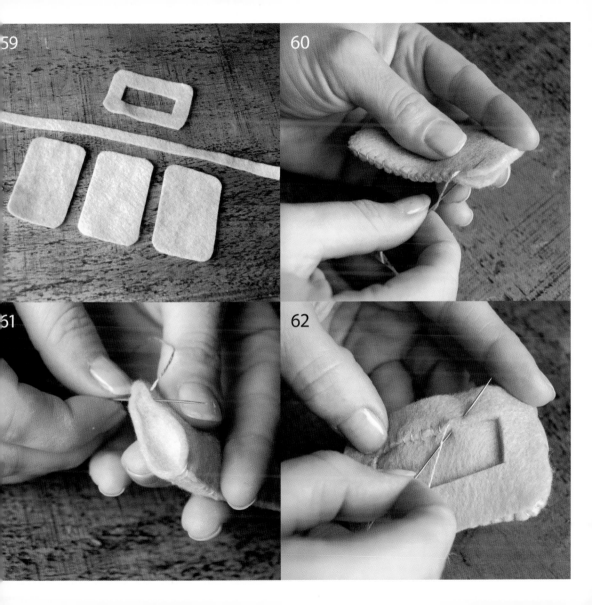

Transfer the pattern from page 27 on to a piece of stabiliser. Embroider the pattern using straight stitch (p16) for the lines and spot stitch (p16) for the dots (Figs 63 and 64). Pin, then sew the long edge piece to the outer edge of the top biscuit piece (Fig 65).

Sew the last biscuit body piece onto the bottom edge of the edge piece, leaving a small gap for stuffing. Stuff the biscuit so it is soft and full yet still flat. Sew the gap closed (Fig 66).

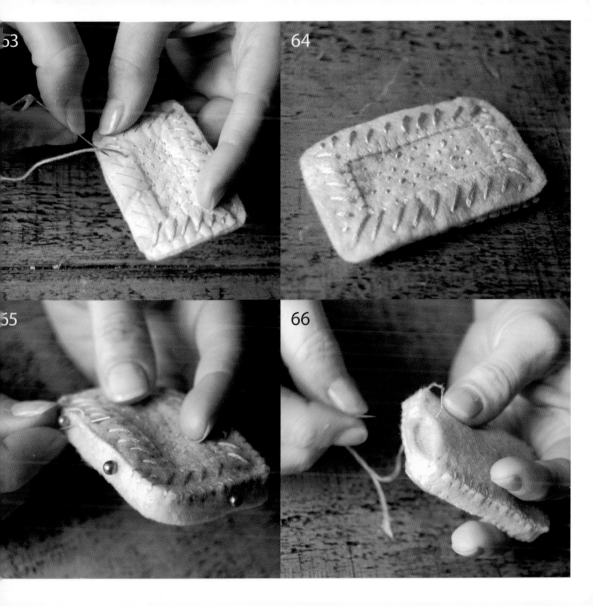

A perfect replica of a shortcake biscuit!

More information from:
↗ **www.nicecupofteaandasitdown.com/
biscuits/previous.php3?item=10**

Pink Wafer

Cut out the 11 pink wafer pattern pieces from page 26 (Fig 67). Pin together the biscuit layers, pinning each to the one below in the following order: pink, 2 x baby pink, pink, 2 x baby pink, pink, 2 x baby pink, pink (Fig 68).

Sew through the stack with a running stitch in a rectangular shape, trying to make sure that the side without the knot is neat, as this will form the base of your biscuit (i.e. the knot should be on the top of the biscuit) (Fig 69).

Transfer the pattern from page 26 on to a piece of stabiliser. Take the spare pink piece, and with the stabiliser pinned to it, embroider all the lines going in one direction using straight stitches (Fig 70). When you've done this, remove the stabiliser.

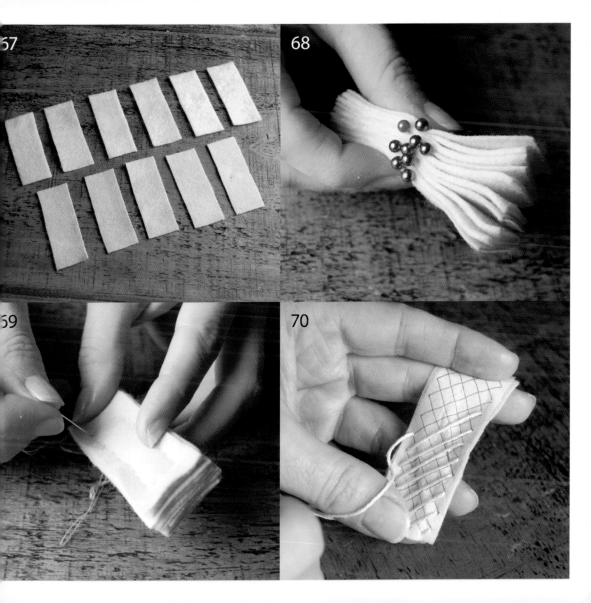

Now embroider the lines going in the other direction. With each stitch weave the needle under and over the stitches going the other way to form a mesh or latticework of diamonds (Fig 71).

Sew this embroidered top piece onto the top of the body stack with seam stitch, with the neat stitching side showing (Fig 73).

OK, it's not a top-scorer on the favourite biscuits poll on the Nice Cup of Tea website (it came top of the 50 yukkiest biscuits!) , but it's still yummy in my book.

Biscuit tin tray

Cut out all 15 of the biscuit tin tray pattern pieces from pages 28 and 29 (Fig 74). Sew the two main pieces together around the outside edges with seam stitch (Fig 75). Sew the four individual edge pieces along the corresponding sides of the rectangular base piece (Fig 76) and then sew up the sides to make up the pink wafer biscuit compartment (Fig 77).

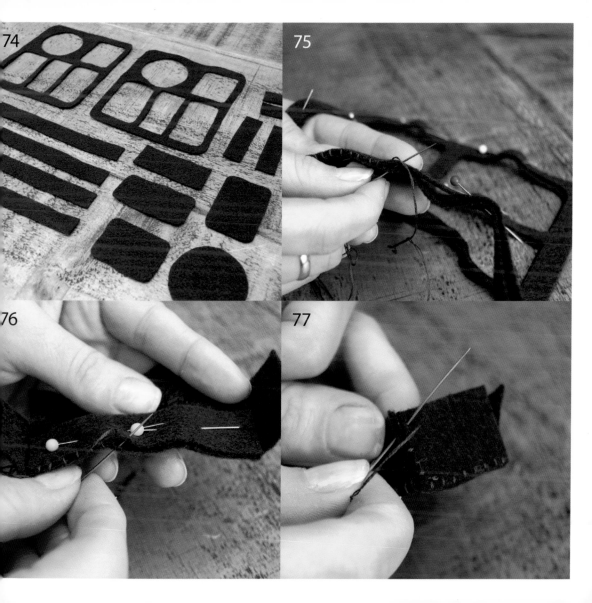

Pin one long edge piece to the edge of one of the rounded-edged rectangular base pieces, taking care to curve the corners (Fig 78). Sew round the edge using seam stitch (Fig 79), unpin and fold up the edge piece to form a container shape (Fig 80).

Repeat with the other three edge pieces, pinning and sewing them to the edges of the other rounded-edged rectangular base pieces.

Pin each of the completed container shapes into its corresponding hole in the tray and sew round the edge using seam stitch (Fig 81). You now have a completed tray (Fig 82).

We'll make the biscuit box next – it is deep enough for two trays so if you'd like to make more biscuits you'll need another tray.

Biscuit tin

Cut out the biscuit tin pattern pieces from pages 30 to 33 (Fig 83).

I thought it might be nice to give the edges of the Union Jack a 'combed' look to break up the line a bit. You obviously don't have to do this if you don't want to but I've described it here if you'd like to get the same look.

Comb the edges of the Union Jack pieces that will form the outside of the flag design (Fig 84). Try combing across the edge as well as towards it. You are trying to break up the edge slightly.

Lay the Union Jack pieces onto the white biscuit tin top piece, pin down and sew round all the uncombed edges using appliqué stitch (Fig 85).

Apply a thin layer of glue to the underneath of the combed edges, using the paintbrush, and pat down (Fig 86). Use as little glue as possible.

Transfer the crown pattern from page 33 onto a piece of stabiliser. Pin the stabiliser onto the centre of the Union Jack and embroider using your gold thread (Fig 87). Use French knots (p24) to replicate the spots on the pattern, stem stitch (p18) for the curved lines and back stitch (p20) for the straight short lines.

Sew the top side pieces together, with the white on top of the grey (so the grey will end up on the inside) to form a strip (Fig 88). Alternate the sizes so they are long, short, long, short.

Sew along one of the long edges of the strip with seam stitch (Fig 89). Then sew the ends of the strip together to form a loop (Fig 90).

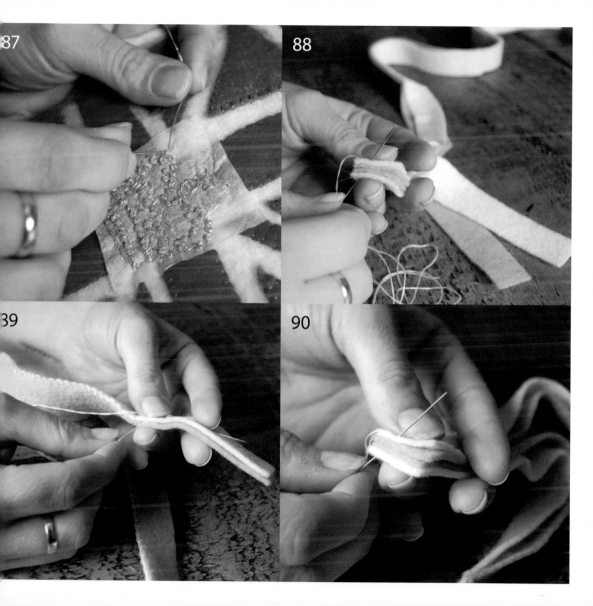

Sandwich the card top piece between the grey felt inner top piece and the embroidered Union Jack outer top piece (Fig 91).

Pin the loop you have just made to the edge of this sandwich and sew around the edge with seam stitch (Fig 92). You now have one finished lid (Fig 93).

Now as you did with the top side pieces on page 72, sew together the bottom side pieces, with the white on top of the grey, to form a strip, so the grey ends up inside. Alternate the sizes so they are long, short, long, short. Sew the two ends of the strip together to form a loop (Fig 94).

Sandwich the card bottom piece between the two grey felt bottom pieces (Fig 95). Pin the loop you have just created to the edge of this sandwich and sew round the edge using seam stitch (Fig 96).

Take the card bottom side pieces and curve both of the short ends of each of them with your fingers to form curves that correspond with the curved corners of the base (Fig 97). Slot the card into the open top edges of the felt sides (Fig 98) and sew the top edge closed with seam stitch (Fig 99).

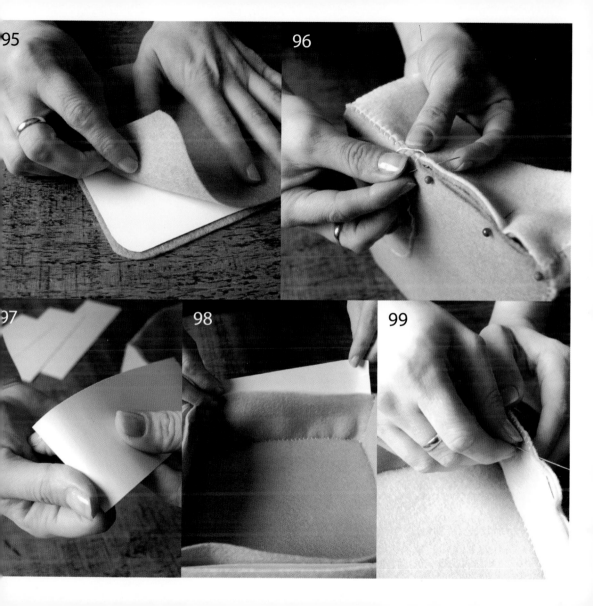

And you're done!

If you'd like to be in with a chance of getting into print with your creations, why not upload a photo of your biscuits here:

↗ www. how2crafts.com/contribute

About the author

Ouissi Gresty loves baking bread, collects champagne corks and can never resist the lure of a bookshop, especially if it contains a teashop. She spends her days with her son and her evenings sewing British foods out of felt.

Her work has been exhibited in galleries, museums and theatres throughout the UK and is sold on various online boutiques.